The Twelve Days of Christmas

Illustrated by Dorothy Stott

Written By: **Kim Mitzo Thompson, Karen Mitzo Hilderbrand**
Illustrated By: **Dorothy Stott** Book Design: **Jennifer Birchler**
Publisher: **Twin Sisters Productions, LLC** Song: **Public Domain**
Executive Producers: **Kim Mitzo Thompson, Karen Mitzo Hilderbrand**
Music Arranged By: **Hal Wright** Music Vocals: **The Nashville Kids Sound**

On the **first** day of Christmas, my true love sent to me **a partridge in a pear tree**.

4

On the **second** day of Christmas, my true love sent to me **two turtle doves** and . . .

On the **third** day of Christmas, my true love sent to me **three French hens**...

On the **fourth** day of Christmas, my true love sent to me **four calling birds** . . .

On the **fifth** day of Christmas, my true love sent to me **five golden rings** . . .

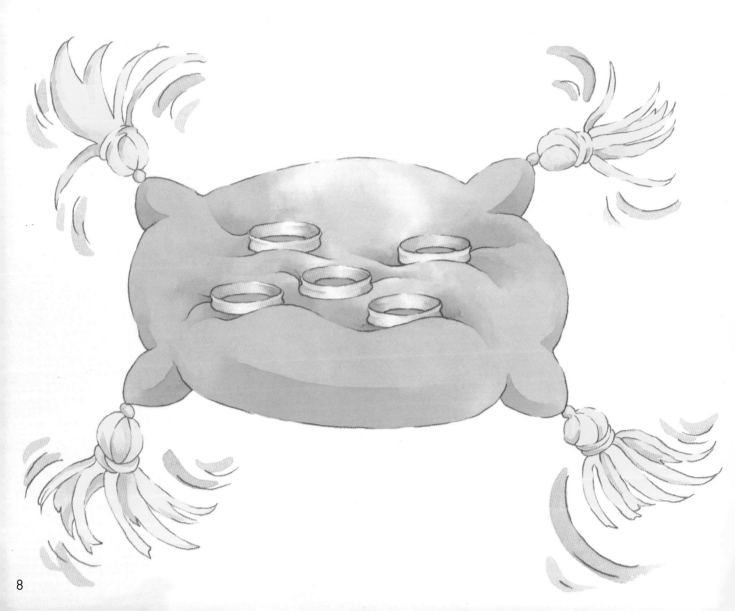

On the **sixth** day of Christmas, my true love sent to me **six** geese a-laying...

On the **seventh** day of Christmas, my true love sent to me **seven** **swans a-swimming** . . .

On the **eighth** day of Christmas, my true love sent to me **eight maids a-milking**...

On the **ninth** day of Christmas, my true love sent to me **nine ladies dancing**...

On the **tenth** day of Christmas, my true love sent to me **ten lords a-leaping**...

On the **eleventh** day of Christmas, my true love sent to me **eleven pipers piping**...

On the **twelfth** day of Christmas, my true love sent to me **twelve drummers drumming**...

Find each of the following words:

Drummers	Ladies	Partridge	Turtledoves
French Hens	Lords	Pipers	Geese
Golden Rings	Maids	Swans	Calling Birds

```
R  I  S  E  E  T  P  G  E  E  S  E
M  A  I  D  S  U  I  F  I  C  M  A
G  E  D  S  W  R  P  E  D  A  O  L
O  L  O  D  S  T  E  F  R  L  P  T
L  D  H  O  M  L  R  R  U  L  A  D
D  L  A  D  I  E  S  E  M  I  R  G
E  G  D  L  S  D  L  N  M  N  T  I
N  R  S  O  P  O  O  C  E  G  R  R
R  G  R  R  I  V  R  H  R  B  I  C
I  L  A  D  I  E  S  H  S  I  D  M
N  R  T  S  E  S  S  E  S  R  G  R
G  S  W  A  N  S  D  N  M  D  E  R
S  I  I  S  R  H  R  S  S  S  G  I
```